Simon's Cat beyond the fence

by Simon Tofield

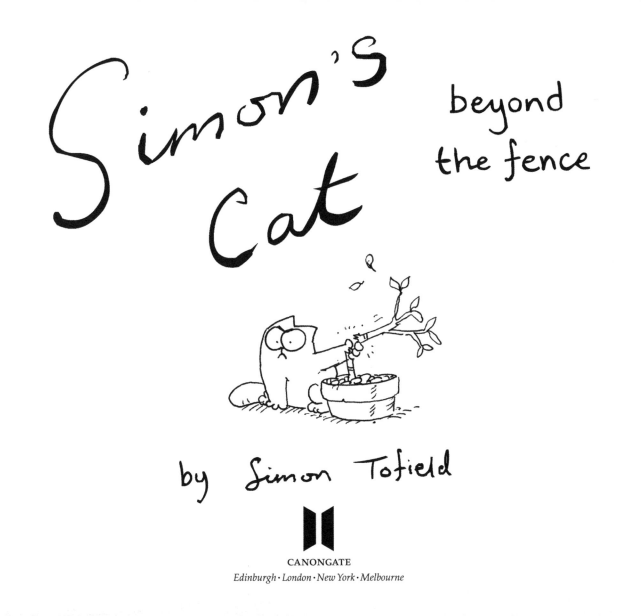

CANONGATE

Edinburgh · London · New York · Melbourne

Published by Canongate Books in 2010

4

Copyright © Simon Tofield, 2010

The moral right of the author has been asserted

First published in Great Britain in 2010 by Canongate Books Ltd,
14 High Street, Edinburgh EH1 1TE

www.meetatthegate.com

British Library Cataloguing-in-Publication Data
A catalogue record for this book is available on
request from the British Library

ISBN 978 1 84767 484 5

Typeset by Simon's Cat

Printed and bound in Great Britain by Clays Ltd, St Ives plc

In memory of my good friend Owain Jones

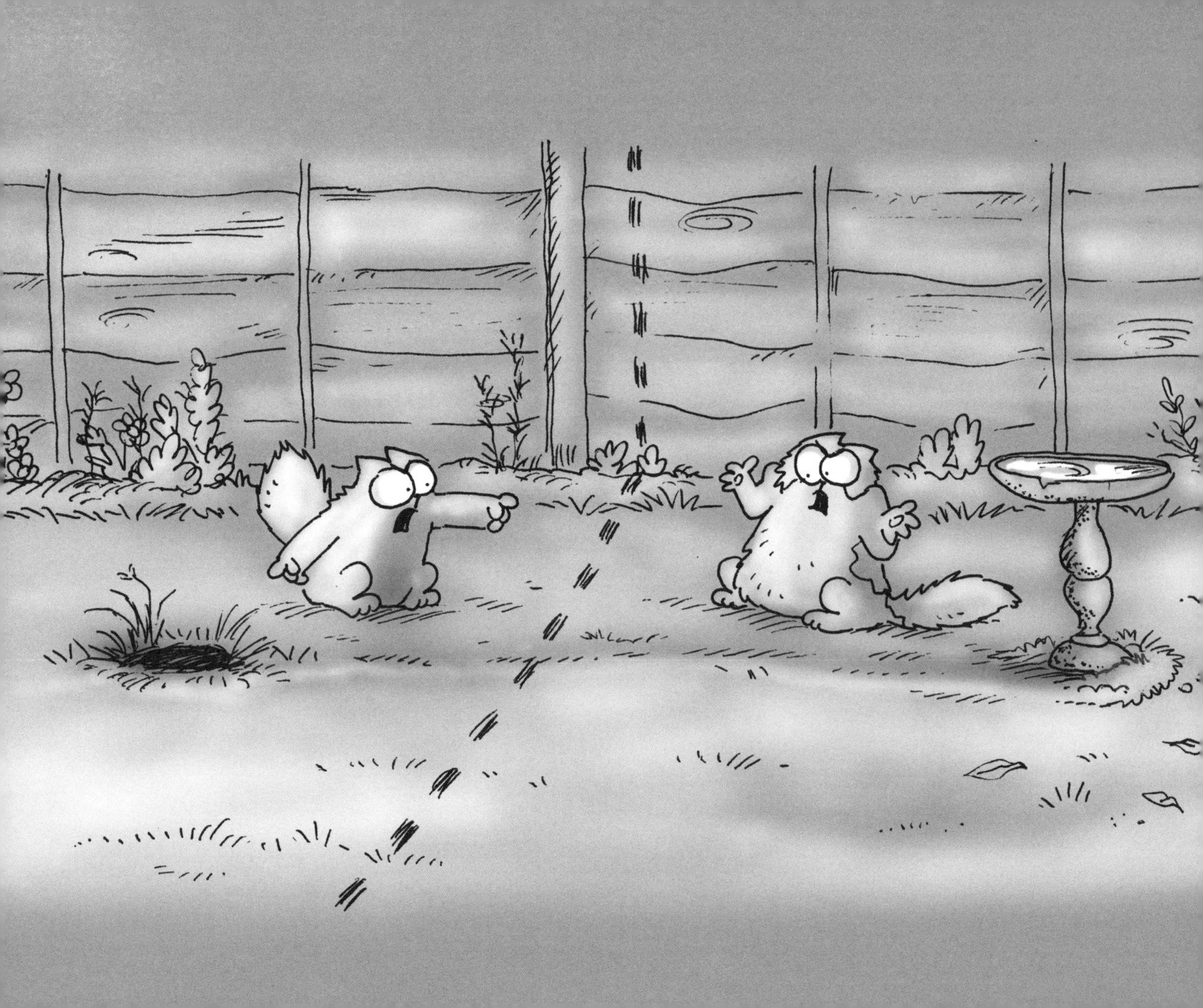

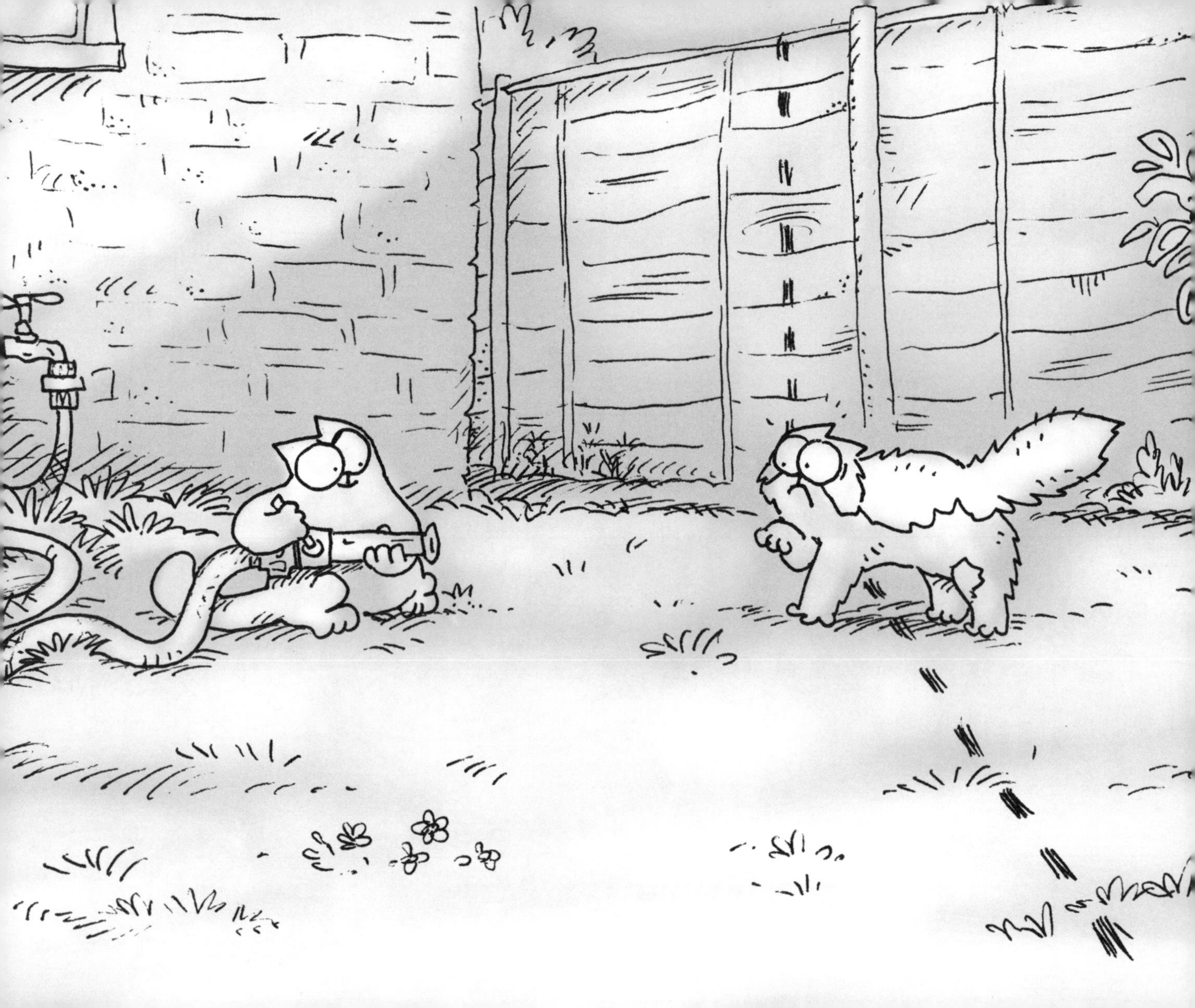

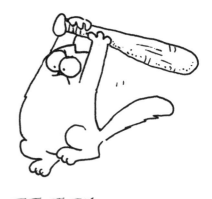

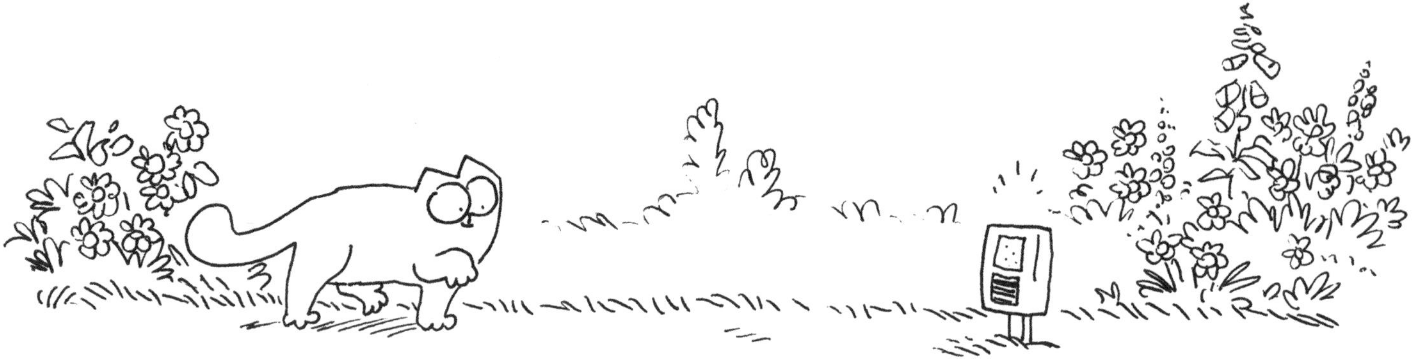

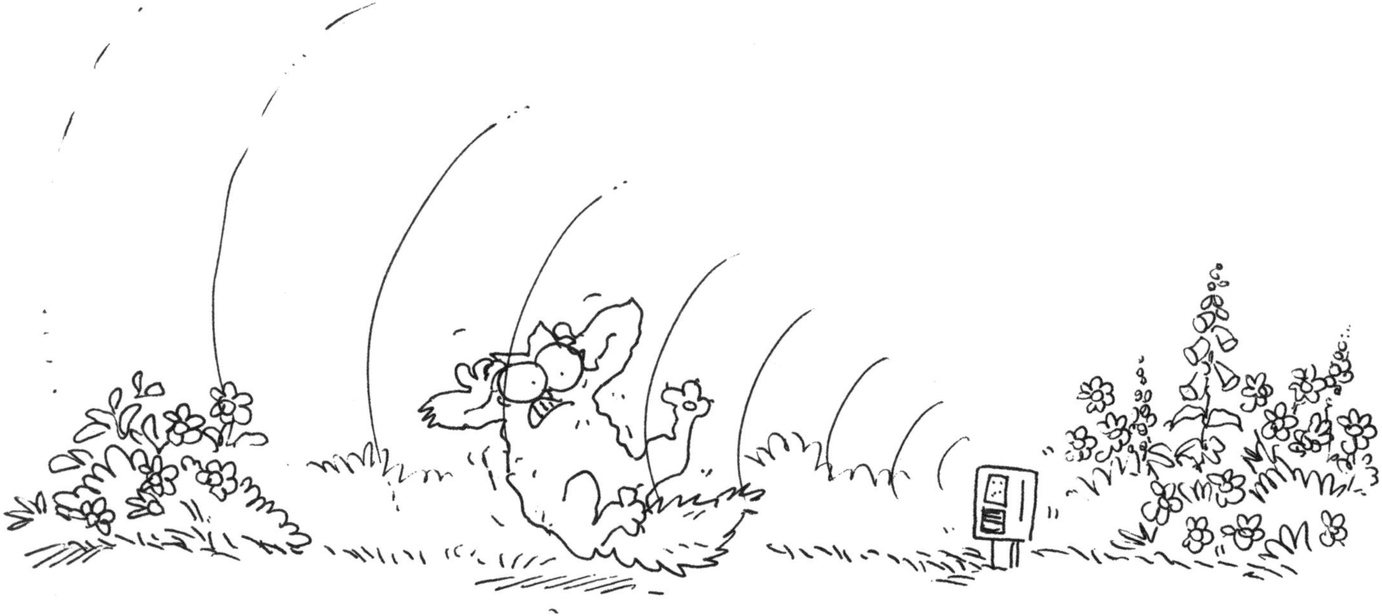

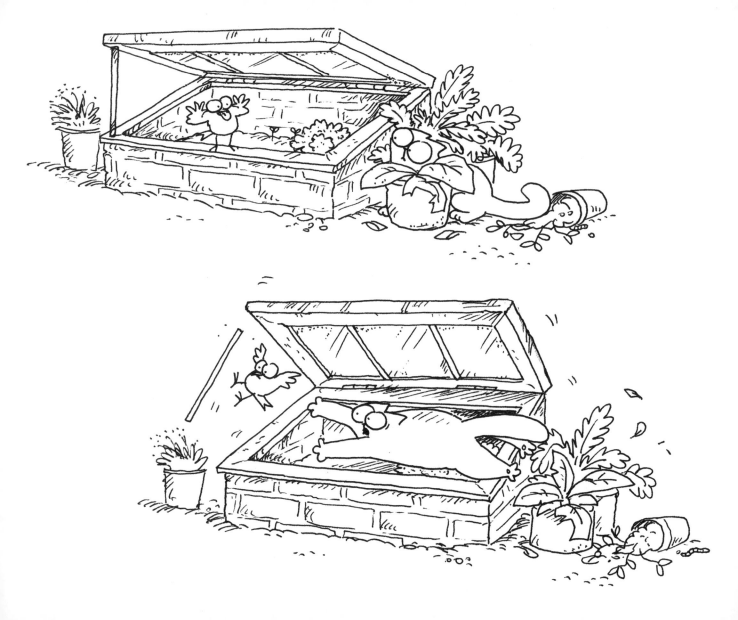

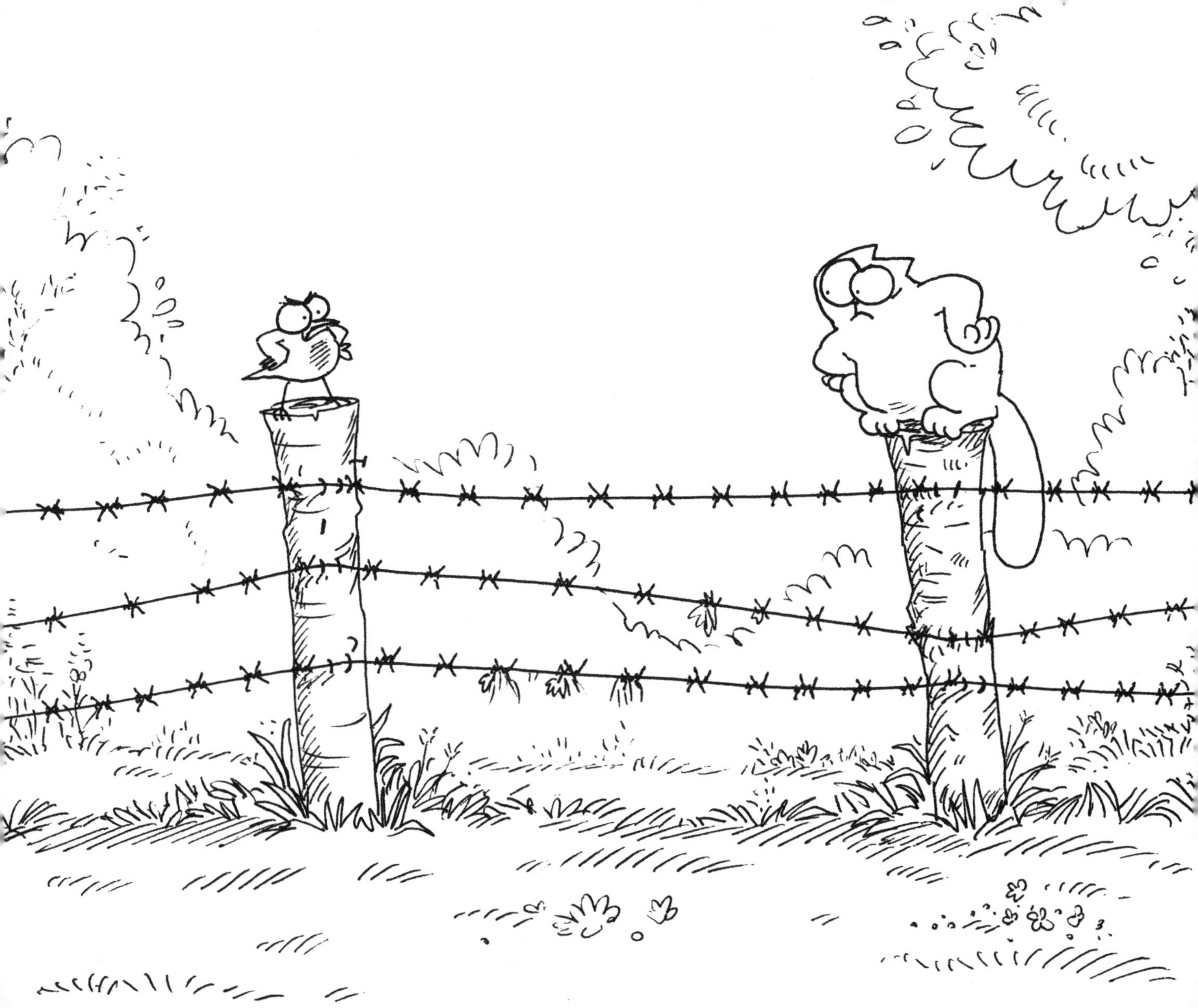

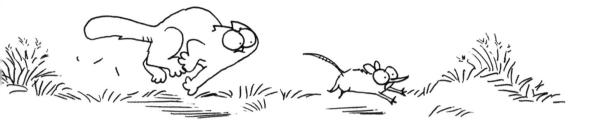

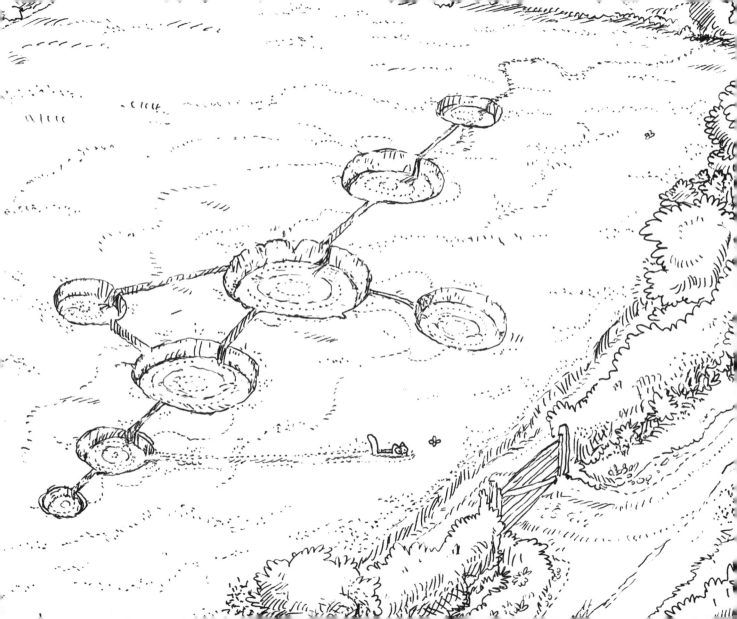

Acknowledgements

Thanks to Kirk Redmond, Don Evans, Martha and Tom Holdom, Barry Geal,
Alan Proctor, Mike Staxman Cook, Matthew and Amelia Shaw, Sean and Kirsty,
Alydia Tobin-White, Sarah and Nick Alexander, Chris Gavin, Sarah and Tim Fancourt,
Walt and Margaret Randall, Nigel Pay, Mike Bell, Daniel Greaves, Mark Burton,
Nick Davies and the Canongate team, Robert Kirby and Duncan Hayes at UA
and my four cats for providing endless inspiration.

For all your Simon's Cat goodies,
check out the webshop at

www.simonscat.com